TURQUOISE PATCH

A collection of poems

Susan Hardy

Copyright © Susan Hardy 2016

All rights reserved. No part of this publication may be reproduced, stored in a retrieval system, or transmitted, in any form or by any means, electronic, mechanical, photocopying, recording or otherwise, without the prior permission of the Susan Hardy and her publisher.
Susan Hardy asserts her right to be identified as the author of this work in accordance with the Copyright, Designs and Patents Act 1988.

The publishers do not necessarily agree with some of the views expressed, or with the syntax used in this book, which we publish at the request of the author.

*

This edition published in Great Britain in 2016 by
Farthings Publishing
8 Christine House
1 Avenue Victoria
SCARBOROUGH YO11 2QB
UK

http://www.Farthings-Publishing.com
E-mail: queries@farthings.org.uk

ISBN 978 -1- 326 – 69169 -1

June 2016 (f)

DEDICATION

This collection of poems is dedicated to the memory of my late husband Trevor Martin and my only son Bevin Julian Martin. They inspired me in their lifetimes. They continue to inspire.

ACKNOWLEDGEMENTS

The English Department, Hull University, Scarborough Campus:

- Martin Arnold
- Matthew Pateman
- Anna Fitzer
- Catherine Wynne
- Ann Kaegi
- Charles Mundye

Special thanks also to Student support Services

- Diane Murphy-Rodgers - my support worker
- Sue Halkyard – my friend
- The late Sorley Maclean. His poem 'Hallaig' triggered my interest in poetry.

And to David Keane

Also many thanks to Scarborough based Farthings Publishing and its partners David Fowler and Ren Yaldren.

CONTENTS

Chalices	9
Miracle Cure	12
Wolf	14
Music	15
Distant Love	16
Cancer	18
Living Ghost	19
Sea Imagery	20
Chestnut Ward	21
Calling	22
Beckoning	24
Eruption	26
Raaysay	28
Justice	30
Turquoise Patch	32
Celestine Gate	34
Faith	35
Rock	37
Isle of the Roe Deer	40
Absent	42
Mercy	43
Mission Statement	45
Files and Pretence	48
Arrested State	51
Naming Names	54
Mean cold spirit of my mind	57
Magnolia Hell	59

The lightness of your healing	60
Earth	62
Undone by you	63
In memory	64
Man of the Mountain	66
Already	67
Departure	68
Freedom	69
Wings	71
Times	72
Clouds rising	73
Inroads	75
Pain	76
Eagle wings	77
Last breath	79
Circles of Sun	81
200 Light years	82
Wizard	86
In anticipation of Thatcher's death	87
The street	89
Why all the effort?	90
Song to Bobby Sands	92
Henry's song	94
Eagles	96
Desire	97
Futile	98
Polar opposites	99
Final Word	100
Photographs	101

PREFACE

Turquoise Patch is a journey through the overwhelming grief following the loss of both my son and husband through suicide.

The collection of poetry was started in the year 2000 during the time I was divorcing from my second husband.

Through this poetry I have worked through the grief of losing my darling son, Bevin Julian Martin, followed four years later by the loss of my beloved husband Trevor Stanley Martin. Both Bevin and Trevor took their own lives, Bevin in 1987 and Trevor in 1991.

Bevin's ashes are scattered on Holaman Island on the Isle of Raasay in the Western Isles.

Raasay is an island Bevin discovered with his Dad while on a camping, cycling and bird watching trip. Raasay is a spiritual place and some of the poems in the collection were written on the island.

Trevor's ashes are scattered on the Isle of Jura at Barn Hill where George Orwell wrote part of *Nineteen Eighty Four*. Barn Hill was a special place to both myself and Trevor. It was where we saw our first Golden Eagle on one of our many camping trips.

Much of the poetry in the collection is inspired by the beauty and power of nature. The metaphysical quality of some of the poems is influenced by the late Sorley Maclean of Raasay.

The last seven poems in the collection were written by Trevor and Bevin.

Susan Hardy 2016

CHALICES

Chalices is dedicated to my late husband Trevor Stanley Martin. Trevor was the only son of Joyce and Stan Martin of York. I was married to Trevor for twenty-one years from 1970 until 1991. Following the death of our only son Bevin Julian Martin in 1987, Trevor struggled to cope with overwhelming grief and in 1991 made the decision to take his own life.
RIP

Through the meadow
To the mountain.
O'er the mountain
To the sea.
To a land of
Milk and honey.
Where my
True Love
waits for me.

Like the swallow
Like the songbird
Like the eagle
I can see.

Five hundred miles before me
Where my True Love
waits for me.

He knows I'm on my Journey
He knows that I am free
Free at last from Tyranny
My Darling waits for me.

He did not want to leave me
He was called.
He had to go

My Love
My Love
My Darling
Has a Home prepared
for me.

The Fire there
Burning brightly
The hearth all swept
and cleaned.
Waiting, watching, waiting
My Darling waits for me.

The Home upon the headland
The table by the shore
In our land of milk and honey
Our cups do overflow.

Raise our cups
Of plenty.
Place the wand behind
the door.
"Take your cloak off Darling
You're home
You're home
For sure."

The night is now upon us.
The darkness closes in.
"Shut your eyes
My Darling
You're not troubled anymore.

Shut your eyes
My Darling
You're home
You're home
for sure."

*

MIRACLE CURE

In memory of my angel boy Jesse-James who passed away July 13th 2015.
Rest in Peace darling boy.

A miracle occurred
the other day
My Darling boy
Walks again.

Free of pain
He walks again

I never thought
I would see
My Darling boy
Walk so free.

I never dreamed
We would go
to the park
to the lake

Had lost all hope
Resigned myself
to his Death
could only drag himself
around the block

One day his Demise
will come
Until that day he walks so free.
My Darling boy walks with me.
My Darling boy walks so free.

My faithful dog
Walks with me.

*

WOLF

We rested a while
On the park bench.
Along she came.
Slowly
A small bent figure
Appeared on the path

As she passed by
The Wolf at her back
She spoke these words;

"Do not be afraid
He will not harm you.
He may look fierce
but he is as gentle as
any lamb."

When they were gone
They left in their passing
A great sense of Peace
A knowing
All is well.

*

MUSIC

'Music' refers to an experience which occurred on the morning following my son Bevin's death.
The music we heard seemed to come from the Heavens.

We stood.
Transfixed by the sound.
The Beauty of which
Transcended Human words.

In the half light of Morning.
That time between
Dark and light.

The sound flowed through
our bodies
Pure White Sound
Filled with Love

The Sound of Love
Filling the sky.
A Gift of Love
of Peace
Harmonious Sound

*

DISTANT LOVE

I Love You
You know that
don't you?

Still do
as a matter of fact.
Still do.
In spite of your marriage
to another.
I still Love you
Always will.

You were sent for
a reason.
To fill a deep need
To heal the pain
To bring harmony
To bring peace.

You are a Healer
A Friend
You are Special.

The Living Ghost
lives on.
Still searching
Still looking for Answers
that cannot be answered.

Toil on weary soul.
Toil on.

You are truly
Deserving.
Of Happiness.
Of Peace.

For You are Special.

*

CANCER

(Dedicated to my sisters Jilly and Janie)

This is the beginning
The cycle without end
The endless painful journey
The cycle starts again.

Weary oh so weary
The mind cries out
In pain.
This lonely cruel journey
Suffering without end.

Yet through the pain and suffering.
Through the veil of tears
Our strength will take us forward
Our light
Will not be dimmed.

We will strive
to touch the sun.
stay resolute and strong
For this is the beginning
Our journey never ends.

*

LIVING GHOST

I am emerged
I am reborn

From the black confines
The cold hard Earth.
I am reborn
I am risen
Alive.

Living Ghost
Journey on, journey on.

Dark to light
Day has triumphed over night.

Rising
Ebbing
The tides continue.
The wrack of grief
Washed
Refreshed.

Ride the Tempest
Never rest
Living Ghost
Of the past.

*

SEA IMAGERY

Flat
Calm
Stagnant

No movement
No tides
Dead sea
No life
No turning of the tides

Tumultuous sea
Raging sea
Hurling forth its foam.

Murderous sea.
Magic sea.
Raging, raging storm.

No calmness
No respite
No resting on a wave

Raging sea
Dead sea
No harmonious middle ground.

*

CHESTNUT WARD

Out of the Blackness
Out of Despair
I screamed very loud
To get my voice heard.

An animal howl
A piercing scream.
Way off the scale
of intolerable
Pain.

I speak really quietly
I feel very weak.
Yet the silence is broken
I now had to speak.

People are listening
They are hearing my Voice
Struck dumb by despair
Now able to speak.

*

CALLING

Calling
Calling
Calling my name.

My Island of Love
Is calling again.

I need you
I need you
to cry out my pain.

The calling is strong
It calls out my name,
My Island of Raasay
Calling again.

I've done what I could
the stone is all set
My Island is calling
Calls me to rest.

I need you
I need you
To cry out my pain.

My Island of Raasay
My Island of Love
Calling my name
My journey for answers
has come to an end
The spirits are with me
They lift me along
My spiritual ancestors

Journey above.
The eagle is soaring
Watching for me.

The road to my Island
It is straight
It is long.
I need you beside me
As I journey along.

The door is wide open
The way is now free
to go to the Island
that is calling to me.

I will look to the West
to the stone on the Point
I found all the answers
No longer do doubt.

I am Free
I am Free
Free from this town
Free from the shackles
that once tied me down.

My home is in order
My way is now free
to go to my Island
Calling to me.

*

BECKONING

You beckoned
I came.
You called yet again
Left a print
On my mind
On my soul
Oh land of the living I now
answer your call.

The call of my people
Call from the shore
Echoes within
Reverberates round.

Round my soul
Round my mind
The call of my people
Calling aloud.

You never do shout
You call on the wind
The call of my people
Calling my name.

Oh land of the living
Land of the Free
Land of my people
Calling to me.

I will not resist you
I too am now Free
to answer my people
Calling to me.

The ferry awaits
the ferryman waves
Signals his welcome
to the land of the Brave.

The brave men of Raasay
The brave and the strong
Ring out their welcome
I won't be too long.

I will go to my people
To the land of the Free
To the land of the living
Who are waiting for me.

The call of the Sound
The call of the sea
The call of my people
Calling to me.

I will not resist
I will be on my way.
When the year it is over.
When the work is all done
The call of my people
Setting me Free.
A welcome awaits
As I travel the Sound
On the wave from the Island
to which I am bound.

*

ERUPTION

On the far side of the
Mountain
In the island of the sun
Grey fingers stretch before you
Protection from the gun.

Eyes which watch your
Island
Looked this way
Before.

High up in the
Mountain
They watch events below.

The ancient site of
Wonder
On which you rest a while
Is watched with
Eagle eyes
The danger of the future
Roll back the sand of
Time.

Time
Which saw the suffering
The movement
from the land
has come again to
haunt you.
Roll back the sands of
Time.

A time before the
Clearance
A time which tells a tale.
A time of
Norse and Viking
A time
to stake the land.

The land on which you stay on
is not a
point of view
It is a permanent reminder
of what is
just and true.

*

RAASAY

Time to say
Farewell
Raasay.
The place I've come to know
to love.
Raasay.

With your ethereal charms
Your gentle streams.
Your raging storms.
Your sense of place.
Your Gaelic tongue.
Wisdom pours from every source.

I would walk an extra mile
to touch again
Your warmth
Your smile.
Forever burning in my Soul.
Magic Isle.
You make me whole.

In a world split apart
by death, disease, broken hearts.
You once again give your Soul.
Exude forgiveness.
Play your part
In bringing love to shattered hearts.

You open up the
World
Your death
Your pain
Turns to me.

I will absorb
with my last breath.
Your hope of
Everlastingness.

*

JUSTICE

They say I am Bad.
They say I am Mad.
They scowl and they frown.
Turn their backs
Walk away.

I am not even sad.
I am really quite glad.
My mind is now set.
I am Focused.
I am Strong.
I suffer the wrong.

I have come through the war
Make my plans to go far.
From their scowls
To a place that is Just.
To a place I can trust.
To a land faraway.

A land joyous and gay.
A land that is free
from the scowls.
From the frowns.

From those who have
Turned their Hatred on me.

The Battle was long.
My mind remains strong.
I will go from this place.
I will not turn to face
those who still doubt.

Those who still shout.
"You are Bad.
You are Mad."

For that is their song.

I will go sing my song
as I journey along
I will go sing of hope
Of Justice
Of Pride
Of Freedom from hatred
With you by my side.

*

TURQUOISE PATCH

I saw a turquoise sea today.
I saw a turquoise sea.
The land was green
The sky was black
The air was pregnant red.
I gulped it down with greedy
breaths as new life stirred in
me.

I couldn't see
I couldn't speak
The silence was profound
Entrapped inside a tomb of
Grief
The poison pumped around.

A dead man's hand reached out to me, he called me
from afar.
Then just in time the Angel came
Restored my inner calm.

Man of woe of times now gone
Leave your love to weep.
New life has sprung from ashes
burned.
Your song is now complete.
My song is ready to be sung
I mourned your loss too long.
Go rest in Peace where-ere
you will.
Tomorrow has begun.

The morning light is breaking now
The waves break on the shore.
The storm has passed
The sky azure
The air no longer red.
I couldn't see but now I can
New life is up ahead.

Restore my strength Angelic One
Restore my strength to me
Then go back to Celestine Gate
Do not wait for me.

I need to see the sea today
I need to touch the shore
I need to walk the waters edge
As I did long ago.

This time for me I walk the shore.
This time I lift my head,
The sight I see is mine alone.
My mourning song is dead.

Twelve years on one day has passed.
One day to call my own
A day of Freedom
From all grief.
The Turquoise Patch has gone.

*

CELESTINE GATE

A promise of the future shore
Upon that Golden Path
An ancient tale revealed briefly
Before the moment passed
Up ahead the ship steamed on
While closer to the shore
The smaller vessel watched in awe
A world of long ago.

We do not need to look too far
To reach our ultimate goal
Cast out the wahoos
from the gaze.
Pathways do unfold

*

FAITH

The Sun is slowly setting
The Journey's at an end
The Epic Journey's over
Now my back can bend.

It's not down to
Jehovah
But belief in me my friends.

It could be I'm a Pagan
My belief in God is nil.
My belief lies in the landscape
A Faith that's deep within.

A Faith beyond all churches
A Faith without a creed.
This natural Faith inside me
fulfils all my needs.

This Faith belongs to no-one
it needs no house of stone
this Faith transcends
pomp and ceremony
This Faith is mine alone.

I cannot name my Faith
I cannot pin it down
Its core is deep within me
It's central to my soul.

This Faith remains my lifeline
while out there on the edge.

Without this Faith I'm nothing
Without this Faith I'm dead.

*

ROCK

About the poem ROCK

The Reverend 'Brimstone' referred to in this poem is a Presbyterian minister who preached his sectarian hatred on the Isle of Raasay for many years. He was the local minister on the Island at the time of my son's death.
My husband Trevor in his innocence asked for him to give a blessing as we scattered Bevin's ashes on Holaman Island. Tallach's reply was shocking; his quote from the bible referring to the fate of those who take their own life offered neither comfort nor compassion.

In this poem I name and shame him.
The following is an extract from a diary Trevor kept for a few months after Bevin's death.

Friday 23 October 1987

'The Reverend 'Fire and Brimstone' would have me talking to myself out there on the Point because his sectarian protocol cannot be satisfied.
"Thou are not of the flock – go from this place and worship your false idols and demi-gods."
"But Father, I mean Reverend, I have no God demi or otherwise. Can ye no' show me a light in all this darkness?"
"Ian warned me about pagans like you. Begone before the fires of Hell consume you also!" (walks dejectedly away).

At least the Orange bigots and the Green bigots have found something to agree about. Oh my eyelids hast thou the stamina for an eternity. TM'

ROCK

You were my Rock
My main Man
You were my Rock
You rolled away
I needed Love
I was alone.

Red Rock of the Mountain
Pure white grain of sand
From Mountain
to the shoreline
innocence. Truth. Beauty
Persecuted land.

Fire
Lightening
Flooding
Murder
Sin
Within your Edenic Garden
The Devil entered in
He preached his hate and loathing.
He walked among your flock
Within his tower of hatred.
The black cloaked
'Reverend Brimstone'.
Talked in tongues his
Loathing
The innocent answer back

Your hatred counts for nothing
Your acts of hate of war
Your stealing, burning, killing
Your child abuse
No more.

You are the Devil incarnate
You will never take the land
From the Good
The Pure
The Innocent
They have gained the upper hand.

Red Hand of the Mountain
Pure white Dove of Peace
Protect this land Forever
Protect the Good, the Meek

Evil dwelled among you
Devil here on Earth
He will burn in Hell forever
You will be left in Peace.

Enjoy your little Eden
Your Ancestors dwell within
The passion of your Dying
Ensure you
Live again.

Red Hand of the Mountain
Pure white grain of sand
Rest in Peace my Darlings
You two will rise again.

*

ISLE OF THE ROE DEER (PEACE)

A Monument stands
To those who were wronged
A symbol of Hope
A new and Just land.

Your fire burns brightly
Your light still shines on
While those that abused you
are consumed in their Hell.

Their unspeakable crimes
Their inhuman acts
Have ensure their committed
There's no turning back.

They are endlessly wandering
Never to rest
They made Hell their choise
They feathered their nests

When the fires of Hell
Are finally damped down
The Ice Age will come
To seal up their tomb.

Bring on your Fire
For we have the Ice
We are steely and cold
We survived the dark night

We may have been starved
Turned out in the cold.
We huddled in circles
Talked of our foes.

We are the survivors
Our Circle ensures
We are protected forever
No-one will breech
The Ice and the Fire
We honed with our teeth.

*

ABSENT

Your card stands out by its
Absence
The empty place where it
should stand.
Marks the difference now
between us
Live your life in your different land.
A land uncaring
Cold, indifferent
Unconcerned for those you
Loved
Stay untroubled by our suffering
Live your life in your different land.

*

MERCY

(Dedicated to Danni Haigh)

These are the tough realities
They are Joey, Marie, Chrissy and
John.
These are the children
This is their song;

The life we were born to
has made us real tough.
Our bed was a manger
Cobbled from dust.

Born in the fall of the Thatcher years
We learnt very early
To hold back the tears.

We think we are normal
this is our life
The parents who bore us
Don't give a shite.

They think that they love us
Their love is our lot
The love which they show us
They don't give a jot.

For family commitments
For boundaries set
For values to live by
Which kindle respect

They're our parents you see
They pretend that they care
For our health and well-being
and with them we share.

The value they've put
On their drugs and their vice
Our parents you see
don't give a shite.

The culture which bores us
Hate their own lives
The culture we live in
The culture of strife

Has stolen from us children
A sense of self-worth

We are tough.
We are angry.
We don't need your care.
We accept with a smirk
This life is not fair.

We stand by our Cross
This Cross that is life
We don't hold a hammer
We don't hold a knife

We hold only hatred
For societies goals
We are the children whom
Mercy
Left out in the cold.

MISSION STATEMENT

(Dedicated to all those maimed and killed in Iraq)

Control is the Mission
Control is the name
The keyword to use
In the malevolent game.

Control of the people
Control of the land
Control of the money
Control of the Mind

The state of the people is in
dire straits.
The statement of many
is that it's too late.

This land it is dying
It once was so free
Now freedom of movement
Is just memory.

The minds of the people
are controlled by the drugs
By drink and diseases
By material goods.

The circle is closing
The policeman stands by
To work to the orders
Issued on high.

The Police State is here
No fucking about.
The fascists have landed
Please get Blair out.

Out from behind
His arse of a wife
From corruption from Bush
and his Iraqi strife.

We struggled for answers
We're British you see.
We struggle for answers
of how this can be.

We are a Nation in conflict
but this one's too big.
We are caught in the crossfire
of bullies made big.

By their greed for the money
the oil and the land
of people so poor they
can now barely stand.

Stand up to bullies
To corruption
To greed
Rise up a Nation
Brought low to her knees.

This land was a free land
Blair sort it out
You have traitored your
People with your ego and greed.

You welcome the bullies
They make you look big
You deny to your people the
Freedom to live.

We are a nation in conflict.
You have brought to our shore
The Malevolent Hatred
Of the
Iraqi War.

*

FILES AND PRETENCE

The system has failed
serves but a few.

Shuffled aside
Labelled as 'Loss'.
Go through the motions
End up as dross.

Paperwork done
Dotted and tee-ed.
Filed under 'Hopeless'.
'Exclude'
'Don't resurrect.'
Open the trapdoor let this one pass.

All in the files
Covered and backed
No case to answer
Cover the tracks
Underworld waits beneath the
Trapdoor.
Drugs and destruction
Paedophiles prowl.
Around every corner awful dead smiles.

'Come here my lovely
a nice place to rest
just take this syringe
sleep and forget.
There's lots more to come
You don't need to work
Just lay on your back

It won't even hurt!
There now it's over
Take pills for the pain.
Come back tomorrow we'll do
It again.'

Black out the pain
with tablets and drink
The fall from the wire won't
leave a dent.

No one will notice
the files are in place
Above the trapdoor the coffin awaits.

Driven away
Dead of night
Extinguished forever
Innocent life

Another statistic
Pretend that you care.
Rubber stamp with a reason
Another dared.

Back in the office.
Pull down the files.
Take the basement.
In future times.

Looking for answers
beneath all the dust.
A kernel of knowledge .
Let's make amends for
those who they fucked.
With their Files and Pretence.

*

ARRESTED STATE

The verdict is 'Guilty'
The sentence is passed.
Guilty of Treason
Betrayer of Love.

You determined to rob from
the day you stepped in
I welcomed you
with your innocent looks.

I should never have married
I knew on that night the
Forces around me
were trying to shout;

'Don't do it Sue
Don't marry this snake.
He's not a Prince on a bike
who can lift you from
grief.
He's a robbing abuser
just stop and think.'

I couldn't back out
the plans were in place.
My family
My friends
all wanted this.

They wanted me happy
They wanted me safe
to marry this man
whose surname was Hate.

Robbed and abused
Hand over hand.
No-one believed me
Now understand.
That the man I had married
Was abusing my love.

They thought me real hard
Thought I was harsh
When out of frustration
I would sometimes shout;
'You're a child
not a man
stunted forever
from the loss of your Mum.'

I tried to sit down, to talk
it all through.
To talk to the man who
had done this to you.

You locked it inside you
put it aside
played on your bikes
played in the yard.

Peter Pan I nicknamed you
for that is your name.
Your mates they all loved you
to them you were great.

Always so eager
Always so keen
to play with your toys,
to remain in a state.
Of perpetual childhood
Of Arrested State.

*

NAMING NAMES

Naming names
I now hit back

History speaks
Records tell
Evil actions
Devil man.

Devil spawn
Devil man

Saw my Home
Saw my land
Saw the records in his hand.
Conspired together
Made your plans

Talked in tongues
Brought the drugs
Summoned Terry from his bed
Like a lamb he went with you
Warped his mind with your drugs.

Turned that night
White to black
From that night no
going back.

Gripped by Evil
Gripped by Hate
Terry Hart he
Sealed your fate.

Forces of Evil
Entered in
Nightmare madness
Now begin

Controlled
Conspired
Poisoned
Killed.
Vice like grip
Held you entrall.

Turn the Evil
Call his name
Weave your hatred all around.

Together plotted my demise.

Walked the night
Incanting Hate

Devils disciple
here on Earth.

You had it all.
You wanted more.
Naming names you knew the score.

You tinkered with my car
I know
Don't deny it
I know for sure.

On the Road

I had to leave, I had to go.

On that day I almost died
The car it rattled
The car it shook
My darling boy knew he must
protect his Mum.
My dear, dear Woody
Saved my life.

RIP Woody Dog

*

MEAN COLD SPIRIT OF MY MIND

Mean cold spirit of my mind

Stranger in the night you come
To settle conflict
To ease the fight.

To heal the wounds
To soothe the way
To face the pain of another day.

Days once gone
cannot return
Yet the pain still haunts
The pain remains.

Haunting
Haunting
Lightening strike
Through the head
Down to the heart.

My love, my life
Husband
Son
Pain and loss
Never gone

Lay quiet
Still.
Rest a while
Mean cold spirit of my mind.

*

MAGNOLIA HELL

I've come back from
Magnolia Hell
Into a world of light.

I've come back from
Magnolia Hell
I'd almost lost my sight.

I've come back from
Magnolia Hell
The crash began the fall.
Couldn't speak
Couldn't tell.
My head had split apart.
For nine long months
Magnolia Hell
Rebirths about start.

I walked into my house of love
Sank down to my knees.
Home again.
Home at last.
Now my heart can bleed

Both head and heart
can heal again
Now I've reached my home.

I've come back from
Magnolia Hell
I've come back
Sane again and whole.

*

THE LIGHTNESS OF YOUR HEALING

(Dedicated to David, Reiki Master)

One spoken word.
One thought so pure.
Connects
Two souls
Twinned
Divine.

I receive the gift of healing
I feel the power within
Your light is like a fire.
Carried on the wind.

The fire first warms the
Coldness.
Then sears throughout my
Soul
It cauterises the pain.

Time is not an issue
Nor the distance of the miles
Nor the work while on the
Journey
For your mind connects with mine.

I feel your presence with me
Your voice
Your touch
Your smile
Your quirky sense of humour
For your mind connects with mine
I feel the Healing Power
It's deep within my soul
Your warmth
Your love
Your energy
For your soul connects with mine.

*

EARTH

The Earth has spoken again today
'A better world is on its way.'

Paintings in the sky, the clouds
Whisper
'Promise'

Tree reply.

Against the odds the knife of hate
has fallen from their grasp;
buried in a sod of earth,
a relic of the past.

The sky reflects the joy and pain
A silent tear is shed.
Sacrificial lamb of peace
Red drops of blood has bled

The gun of love
Fires across
The Bloody path of Hate
Rebirth
Renewal
Regenerate
A testament to Fate.

*

UNDONE BY YOU

That night in early Autumn
in the shelter by the playground.
Where I had played as a child

I was undone by you

Pressed against the hard cold bench
Unable to move.

I was undone by you

As a child I had played so free
Swing on swings
Sat on see-saws
Played around
Until that night

Undone by you

From that night my needs
had changed, the swings held no appeal.
The see-saw even less

My ups and downs from
that dark night
reached new heights
plummeted new depths

*

IN MEMORY

(Dedicated to the memory of Peter, loved by many, who died of cancer before completing his degree.
Awarded an Honorary Degree in recognition of his work both as an academic and humanitarian. His tireless work with animals continued after his passing.
RIP

Cast back our mind to early days.

Frightened
Confused
Yet still amazed.

The love which dwells within
these walls;
gave us strength
made us hold

That one small light
Which guides our way
Belief
In us from those who knew
We would aspire

He brought the flame
He touched the fire

The light grew dim
The light grew dense
That light of hope
Almost extinct.

Clung together
Loosing hope
That light of hope
Still dimly shone
Our strength of will
almost gone.
That light of hope kept us strong

That light of hope
Will never die
Within these walls
The meek do fly.

*

MAN TO THE MOUNTAIN – WOMAN TO THE SHORE (GAELIC PROVERB)

A simple stone
thus inscribed
watch over

Dun Caan

Mountain
See
Mountain
Know
Witness
Protect

Watch over

Dun Caan

Lie quiet gentle Son
Lie peaceful

You are home.

*

ALREADY

Already
The dawn of ecstasy unfolds
Already
doubts begin to form.

Already
Howling wolf
Alone
Bay to agony
at the moon.

Alone and agony
familiar friends
Alone and agony
walk away.

Moon shines down
guides their way

Untouched by man
Wild and free
Their grace
Their spirit
A terrible beauty.

*

DEPARTURE

So soon
'Time'
has come
to say

Farewell

Fare
Well

Two words combined
Two souls entwined
Two separate
Two grow
Nurtured
with words truly said

Fare
Well

*

FREEDOM

Can it be true
Can it be real
This feeling I have
Free of all pain.

Can I be certain
Can I be free.
This love that I feel
can never love me.

The pain of the journey
Has come to an end
The love dreaming beside me
has made my heart mend.

Freedom is precious
It goes beyond words.
You may lay here forever
Entwined in your love.

Keep the twine loose
don't tighten the knot.
For Freedom from pain
that rule is a must.

Lay here beside me
for Freedom is love.
These words I now give you
to keep for your own.

Keep them forever
Forever to hold.
As your journey moves onwards
you'll journey alone.

Your life won't be lonely
Nor lacking in love,
but wholesome, rewarding
I give you my love.

It's given with nothing
No strings and no ties.
No catches or clauses
Love makes you fly.

Fly on your own
but come back sometime
Your life's rich with freedom
The freedom of love.

*

WINGS

Lost in the melee of childhood.
Frozen in time and in space.
A pupil formed in the fifties
Has emerged serene and with grace.

'Grace'
a state locked inside us.
'Serene'
a more visible face.

Confined
in a gossamer covering
Fragile
with little defence.

Butterfly
spreading her wings
soars
to her heavenly heights
Up to the temple above her
Gracefully
meeting with fate.

Her beauty outshining all others
Her tranquil life on the earth,
has passed beyond all knowing
to enter a state of
Rebirth.

*

TIME

Time we spent together
now time we spend apart.
Time is all it takes
to heal a broken heart.

Time to heal is special
Healing is the key
Special time together
We set our spirits free.

Free and wild to wander
Spirits walk with me
Gently, calming, perfect
We walk in harmony.

The path I trod was lonely
Painful, cruel, hard
Yet the insight which you gave me
I've come to recognise

The eagle came to find me
He gave me strength to see.
Now wisdom, love and courage
Will always walk with me.

Soaring in his glory
His eyes shine down a light
Seeing all and knowing
A special time apart.

*

CLOUDS RISING

Every cloud has a silver lining
Every sorrow has its place.
Every song has several meanings
All the pain won't go to waste

Waste the pain
Waste the meaning
Waste the suffering
Waste the hurt

Don't be angry with your losses
The gains will come if you just wait.

Your friends are there
just go and find them
some people seem so full of hate.

Just turn your back
shrug your shoulders,
then show again a smiling face.

Don't take the flak for others sorrows
When they turn round and show you hate.
Tell yourself the love you're feeling
Will get you through to find a meaning
Then show again a smiling face.

For life is laughter
Life is sorrow
Life has meaning
You'll make it work.

Your life for you does have meaning
Love yourself
Your life has worth.

*

INROADS

There are many roads to the heart

The long
The smooth
The fast
The sure
The road to choose for those who know
The harder journeys not for them
The one of choice for many men.
That roads have travelled many times
It's kept in perfect repair you'll find.
There are those who need fast-track.
A quick trip to the heart and back.

The other roads much harder now.
Dusty, dark, bumps and bends.
It takes more skill to drive this road

Intuition
Maps and goals.
Take your time on this road.
This road called life is long and hard.
This road for those who slow right down
For those who look and take their time.

This road's for those who in the end,
Rest within their journeys goal.
A gentle heart of Peace and Love.

*

PAIN

Red hot Pain
Soars through my veins
The gun of love
has fired again

The way was sure
The way was right
The gun of love has fired tonight

That fatal shot
has left me floored
Another death
Another road.

Lead me forward
Lead me there
To the touch
To the smell
To the place
Which once was Hell.

*

EAGLE WINGS

You came to say;
Your wings await
goal achieved
You're about to leave.

You're about to soar
You're set to fly.

Their Eagle Wings
In earthly terms
You achieved
Starred first

With this award
You've reached a state
of Angelic Grace.
Ascended to a Divine state.

The celebrations about to start
Your fledgling flight
on baby wings
brought you here
to your Mum.

You came last night
You came to stay
"Look Mum, what he gave."
A gentle son who made the grade.
"Take care son on your wing.

Those wings are rare and precious tools.
Keep them safe
With those wings you'll soar to heights.
Beyond all reason
Beyond all doubt

Those wings of yours are six feet long
With those wings you can't go wrong.
Enjoy those wings
Perhaps one day
You might fly past so I can say.

That's my son
Up in the clouds
That's my boy
Who now can fly.

Flying over, flying by
My darling son flies on high."

"It's easy Mum
It's easy now
I've worked so hard
Now I can fly."

Majestic Eagle
Circling high
Majestic Eagle
Soaring by.

*

LAST BREATH

(Last breath was written during the long process of an organ retention inquiry. This was conducted by Helen Rickard, head of operations at the National Bereavement Partnership. I would like to thank Helen for her tireless work which resulted in a successful outcome to this inquiry.
Thank you Helen. You gave me peace. You listened. You understood.)

My son's ashes are scattered here
A victim of the Thatcher years
Destroyed his mind with their plans.
Their vision of a promised land.
Laid his body on a slab
ripped apart this young lad.
Set in resin parts of him
Committed crimes
the worst of sins.
Stole from him those
vital parts.
Left me with a broken heart.

They never told me of their plans
to do this deed to this young man.
They never told me what they found
In that closed tomb deep underground.
I need to know
They had to say (in layman's terms.)
just what they found

I won't give in until they return
those tiny parts that make the whole.

You'd better tell
I'll shout it out
I'll take you to the
Court of Rights
In Europe's name
Now spell it out.

Your evil ways
begs belief
You lied
You lied
Through your teeth.

Tell the truth
then give me back
the body parts which you stole

You ripped them out
You ripped my soul.

I'll fight bare-handed
To the death.
I'll fight this cause with
My last breath.

*

CIRCLES OF SIN

Come little girl
Come, come, come in.

Very pretty,
Very pure,
Ripe to pluck
Come little girl
in this circle you will see;

a world removed from all you know.
A world wrapped inside a shield of hate.
Enter now.
Hate guides your way
Enter through
The paedophile gate.

This secret world
(it's name is sin)
Takes the young
The pure
The good
Stains their lives
With the foul corrupt
Paedophile knife.

*

200 LIGHT YEARS
(Four Feathers)

(Remembering events of 2000. A Full Moon, a Dog Fox in the garden, Four Magpie Feathers)

One for sorrow
Two for joy.
Three for a girl
Four for a boy.

When Magpies feathers fell that day
I looked and listened did they say,
"These are the symbols of the joy.
The sacred sun has sent the boy.
Go to the place where he stays.
The question mark will be erased.

First you must get a dog that is faithful,
loving and good.
He will guide you through the maze.
He'll sit with you as you gaze.
He'll be your friend through thick and thin.
Your epic journey now begins."

I gathered roses
Made my plans
Took the cards
in my hands.

They spoke of many things that day
The Tower
Lightening
Flashing flood
Sun and Moon
Fighting God

Chariots of Wrath
The stable left with open door.
Lions leapt with fiercesome roar.

I travelled up to whence I came
Moved slowly on
Called your name.

The night was bright
The Sun not set.
He led me on to the place
As she set
I saw your face.

The gentle Moon
gently gazed
with eyes half-closed
she softly sighed
as the miracle did unfold.

The fading Sun
Slowly set
bathed the Earth in radiance.
As the Sun
took her bow
Majestic Moon
Rose on high.

She spoke to me
Called your name
The lovely Son
Was born again.

Though I knew he couldn't stay.
He smiled at me as if to say
"It wasn't for me to disclose the answer

'Why' for which you strove.
You'll find the answer just don't fret.
You have a choice, I had none.
Your silent journey has begun."
With these words he went away
The Sun rose early again that day.

The Roses laid
The Vigil done
I turned the stones
One by one

On those stones
On the sand
I walked again a wonderland.

A voice boomed down, shook my repose;
"Don't look down, look far and wide
What you seek, will be found.
Don't stay too long
Move about
When you're ready
Then you'll shout."

As I am
So are you.
I struggled on
Kept my word
Until the day the Path unfurled.

It opened up
Stretched far and wide
The truth then sought
Now finally found.

The Path I trod
Was smooth and white
I slipped sometimes
I had my doubts
About the sanctity of the plan
To seek the Truth
Entombed by Man.

*

WIZARD

I understand
Lightening
I understand
Bolts
I understand
Swords
I understand
Fire
I understand
Ice
I understand
Dark
I understand
Light
I understand
Chaos
I understand
Calm
I understand

*

IN ANTICIPATION OF THATCHER'S DEATH

You signed your Death sentence
I am not sorry to say
All the Hate
All the Loathing
Means nothing today.

Your vision of Dominance
Your money crazed eyes
Your look to the future
For those of your kind

You plagiarised Francis
yet the animals know
You are the Devil incarnate
The world knows for sure

Your Evil experiments
on both man and beast.
Your disregard for their Nature
The old, sick and weak.

Well the 'lady' will turn
She will writhe
She will scream
as she burns deep in Hell
with those of her kind.

The legacy left here
must now make us see
that never again
the voice of the Fascist
will never be heard.

We are now at 'ground zero'
The World is awash
in the dust of your hatred
Yet we will
Rise up.

The Earth will rise up
The ash will disperse
The poor dispossessed
Will achieve their
World Peace.

*

THE STREET

(This poem is dedicated to Homeless people everywhere. It does not refer to the Youth and Community building in Scarborough with the same name as this poem)

On one leg
She stood
Proud

No complaining
No bitterness
No hate

This life sometimes really hurts
It really cuts you to the quick.
Just a few do care.
For the rest, the sight means nothing.
Not worth a second glance.
They will never share the pain.
Nor experience
Living on the street

They will never see the Human Spirit
Shining through
The mean cold life that is
The Street.

*

WHY ALL THE EFFORT? YOU DON'T LIVE FOREVER

(by Trevor Martin)

Existence is a long and narrow track
Filled with waters deep and black.
From womb to grave
It winds and winds
A lifetime long ago but displays no signs.
A lifelong walk with no guidelines
May as well crawl down the mines.

Amongst those waters still and cold
are many rocks which contain no gold.
Upon those rocks one lives one's life.
Together with kids and wife and strife.
Many people alone.
It's hard to get one's dog a bone.
Every contestant must thrive unaided.

To have to burn is being degraded
And every rock is quite the same
Foul and grimy (hard for the maimed)
One sets off when one can crawl
Exchange one's bonnet for some overalls.
One tramps that track a lifetime long.
Yet no-one seems to think it wrong.
Rules say that one keeps one's self
Slave for the food upon the shelf.
Do not suffer from depression
A day on sick is a week's regression
People race down that slimy road
To see who's best, whose bills aren't owed.

They've completed the walk
They've walked the length
Buck House garden party for the tenth.
Now in time they will die
Just like him or you or I.

They must be proud to be the first.
I really hope they die of thirst.
Their tiny minds must be the worst.
No, work is not my only hate.
I am not a supporter of this state
More people crawling like hordes or rats.
Then they all can buy new hats.
Society is one massive drag
A game to play with luggage tags.
People who like their jobs must be weird.
They enjoy giving orders and to interfere.
They just see a chance to be the boss
It's great for their prestige, they used to be lost.
Listen to that bellow so booming and big.
It must be such fun to mimic a pig.
While the workers below sweat as they dig.
Hoping sometime they will be shouting and smoking a cig.
It must be good to work for their money
To act inferior and respond like a bunny.
But think of the fun when they go and see honey.

They tell her of this and that,
visit the vicar and buy a new hat.
They're so funny.

*

SONG TO BOBBY SANDS

(by Trevor Martin)

On History's page he's earned his place.
The youthful Bobby Sands.
He made his final sacrifice
for the Freedom of Ireland.

His face grew drawn, his eyes fell closed.
Slowly he did die.
Murdered by Imperialists.
Though this they do deny.

They had to justify his Death
to suit their filthy game,
to suckle up to Paisley and
those who are insane.
Insane to think they're kidding us,
they must think I am blind
those Orange thugs and Monarchists
are running out of time.

Twelve years for having firearms
was what they gave this man.
While British soldiers kill and maim
and never give a damn.
They locked him up in Long Kesh jail.
They threw away the key.
But Fermanagh folk said Bobby Sands
would be their next MP.

Bobby's voice was never heard
inside of Parliament.
They screamed he was a criminal.
We heard their anger vent.
They dressed him up in prison garb.
They would not let him see
his fellow Long Kesh inmates of
Irish Liberty

The Hunger Strike is over
for Bobby Sands is gone.
Now he's gone beyond their reach
Beyond their words of hate
Yet I do not doubt the day will come
When six counties are Free
From Union Jacks
The Unionists
From British Tyranny.

*

HENRY'S SONG

(Written in collaboration with Henry Halkyard, aged 8)

B and Bs are for Wimps.
We just sleep rough on our,
    'Sleep when we're dead' tour of Scotland!

We don't need our beds
'Cos we sleep when we're dead on our,
    'Sleep when we're dead' tour of Scotland!

When we're dead on our feet,
We just fall asleep on our
    'Sleep when we're dead' tour of Scotland!

Little Jess fell in love
His eyes are like doves
As he looks on his love, on our,
    'Sleep when we're dead' tour of Scotland!

On the Ferry he gazed
In the eyes of his maid
On the boat to the Island in Scotland.

His girl is a 'gael'
She lives with her 'da'
On the island we love here in Scotland

His dream may come true
To father a few
of his girlie's wee puppies
in Scotland.

He plays in cahoots
As he lives out his days
Here in Scotland.
Now he's no time for sleep
As he lays there and peeks,
At his bonnie young Breya in Scotland.
The seep it will come
Now our travelling's done
As we stay on our island
In Scotland.

*

EAGLES

(by Trevor Martin)

The Pair
Powered by instinct
Their wings brushed
Before soaring gently apart.

They floated
First together
Then next away
As Timeless as
Infinity.

The Earth below obsessed with
a sleep fascination.
I understand not the
Mystery of Freedom.
As these Eagles flew.
With a Universal Oneness

*

DESIRE

(by Bevin Martin)

He comes from a wild land
With long grass and church spires.
We could lose ourselves in the heart
Of the Fire.
Oh how I'd like to lose myself
In his love.

I could tie him to a tree
Lick him into submission.
Only a dream could ever dare
Bring me so close to this
Unholy state.

He's God to me.
He's Godlike
How I pray for him.
His poetry is my Bible.
His words
Daze me
Hold me spellbound
In his Glory

*

FUTILE

(by Bevin Martin)

The medal's a salute
to the soldier so brave
But a medal's no use
pinned to a man in his grave
It stands for nothing
When it stands for the pride
Standing for Death on the fireside.
She lost her love
to the Hate of war.
Sacrificed his life.
And he didn't know what for.

*

POLAR OPPOSITES

(by Bevin Martin)

When the cold blows
It's just a state of mind.
When your girl goes
She's been cruel to kind.

When your hair greys
There's no need to brush them away.
It's just your body's way of saying
Start living from today.

I'm so twisted.
I laugh at people.
People like me.
Twisted people like me.
Find hurting people amusing.

*

FINAL WORD

(by Bevin Martin)

There is many a knife
In many a hand
They would rather kill
Than try to
<u>Understand</u>

      *

Sue Hardy

*Sue Hardy's late husband
Trevor Stanley Martin
who died in 1991*

Left: Sue Hardy's late son,
Bevin Julian Martin
who died in 1987

Below: Jesse James